Teaching the Civil War
with the Internet

Grades 4-12

Internet Lesson Plans and Classroom Activities

A companion Web site for this book is maintained at:
URL: http://twi.classroom.com/civilwar

Teaching the Civil War with the Internet

Internet Lesson Plans and Classroom Activities

classroom
CONNECT
2221 Rosecrans Ave., Suite 221
El Segundo, CA 90245
URL: http://www.classroom.com
Email: connect@classroom.com
(800) 638-1639

Acknowledgments

Senior Product Developer: Kathleen M. Housley
Writer: Michael Headings
Editors: Todd Frey, Tara Houston
Production Designer: Sam Gorgone, Dawn Ranck, Gregory D. Wirt
Cover Design: Nathanael Waite
Manufacturing: Benjamin Cintas

Due to the changing nature of the Internet, site addresses and their content may vary. Great care has been put into the selection of the very best Web sites for this series. But, no long term assurances can be made regarding their suitability for school use. Please visit the companion Web site for this product for updated addresses.

Classroom Connect
Corporate Offices
2221 Rosecrans Avenue, Suite 221
El Segundo, CA 90245

Classroom Connect
Product Development Offices
1241 East Hillsdale Boulevard
Foster City, CA 94404

URL: http://www.classroom.com
Email: connect@classroom.com
(800) 638-1639

All terms mentioned in this book that are known to be trademarks or service marks have been appropriately capitalized.

Printed in the United States of America.

2 3 4 5 6 7 8 9 10 - 02 01 00 99 98

ISBN: 0-932577-68-7

Product Code: TWI-1020

Contents

Lesson Plans: Grades 9-12

Introduction

A familiar comment often uttered by grade school history students is: "Why do we have to study this?" In the past, students learned about history only through the "eyes" of a single textbook company. Today, the Internet makes history come alive for students, and therefore, more meaningful. Instead of just reading a textbook, the Internet gives students access to primary sources such as diaries, historical documents, and speeches of people who actually lived through and witnessed the events they're studying. This allows students to become the primary filter through which understanding is passed.

The resources in this book, such as diaries and actual historic documents, have been selected because they explain history in a first-person manner. The activities in the book help students understand how these historical accounts are important to the development of the United States and to their lives. Experiencing history through the eyes of people who actually lived brings a whole new level of appreciation to its study.

This book presents students with historical views from a variety of perspectives. We see history through the eyes of early colonists, runaway slaves, and immigrants coming through Ellis Island. By examining the actual words of some of these historic people, students can move beyond memorization into analysis and evaluation of their motives. Students can also look at historical events from multiple perspectives. Students will realize that the study of history is much more than learning a string of facts; it is a quest to understand the perspectives, motivations, and actions of human beings.

The study of history also promotes an understanding of how present day issues are related to and have a historic relationship to events of the past. The lessons in this book have been designed to connect events of our nation's history with the feelings, attitudes, and actions of individuals who lived during a particular time. This personal connection will help students better understand the issues that face them as well. Hopefully, it will also help answer the ever-present question: "Why are we studying this?"

Civil War

Grades 4-6

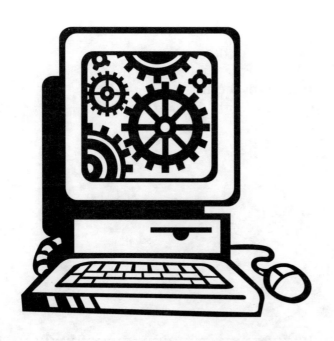

The Firing
on Fort Sumter

Overview

Students will learn about Fort Sumter and the events lead-ing to the firing on the fort in this lesson. They will also be introduced to the controversy surrounding the attack and will write a news article from the perspective of the North and of the South.

Materials

- Computer with Internet access

Objectives

- Research information on Fort Sumter
- Gather information to support the positions of the North and of the South in the firing on the Fort
- Share articles dealing with the impressions of the attack from the viewpoints of both the North and South

 # Procedure

1 This lesson should begin with background information on the secession of the Southern states and the controversy over Fort Sumter. Teachers can start by going to the following Web site:

Secession of States
URL: http://tqd.advanced.org/3055/graphics/experience/
   secession.html

Now have students click on "move on." They will be at the Jefferson Davis site. You can decide if you want them to also have this information. Have students click "move on" again and they will now be at the site on Fort Sumter.

Teacher's Note: This site has hyperlinks that can be clicked on to give detailed explanations of certain vocabulary.

This site gives a brief historic description of the fort on a location map. The teacher should discuss the following points:
• The purpose of Fort Sumter.
• Why it was important to South Carolina.

2 Set the scene for the battle that occurred at Fort Sumter once you have completed the introduction. Explain the following to students:
• The fort lacked supplies.
• South Carolina had seceded from the Union.
• Lincoln wanted provisions to strengthen the fort.
• The South chose to attack Sumter before the supplies arrived.

3 Explain to students that considerable controversy was raised when President Lincoln sent supplies to Fort Sumter. It has been suggested that Lincoln was deliberately trying to provoke the South into firing on the fort, thereby starting the Civil War.

4 Have students open the following Web site:

After Sumter
URL: http://tqd.advanced.org/3055/graphics/experience/
2.html

This site portrays the country's feelings about the attack at Fort Sumter through a quote from the time. Have students read the quote and react to it from the point of view first of a Northerner and then of a Southerner. Have students turn their inferences into the form of a news article using the "North/South" worksheet. Make sure to remind students to incorporate the facts about Fort Sumter they learned from the sites.

Have the class share their news articles when they are done and publish them in the form of a book.

 # Extensions

1 Hold a mock trial in which students must defend or support the premise that the South started the war. Next, put the North on trial. Use the Internet to gather additional information for the debate.

Reflections on Fort Sumter
URL: http://www.tulane.edu/~latner/Reflections/
Reflections_intro.html

2 Students can read a first-hand account about the fall of Fort Sumter in a letter written to a soldier's parents that can be found at the following site:

Haskell Papers, #320
URL: http://ils.unc.edu/civilwar/haskellpg.html

Have students write their own letters back to the soldier with questions and comments they would ask about the battle at Fort Sumter.

4

Lesson Plan   The Firing on Fort Sumter
....
Teaching the Civil War with the Internet

The Firing on Fort Sumter

Student name: _____

Class: _____ **Date:** _____

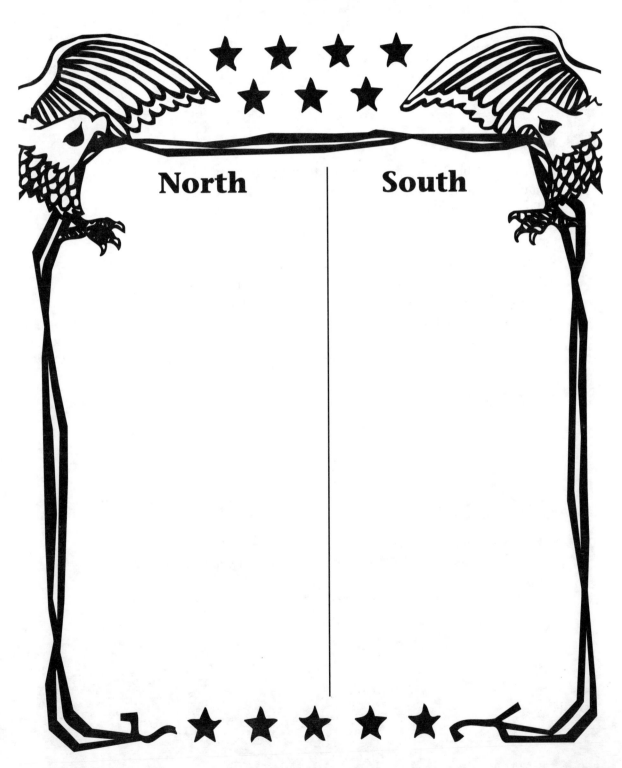

North | South

<table>
<tr><td>

LESSON PLAN

Number 2

</td><td>

Through the Eyes of a Child

</td></tr>
</table>

 Overview

It is often difficult to understand history through the eyes of a child who lived through certain events. This lesson will center around a child named Carrie Berry who kept a diary throughout the Civil War.

Students will read the diary of the ten-year-old girl from Atlanta, Ga., and discuss the diary and the girl's insights about the Civil War. In addition, students will create their own Civil War diary.

 Materials

- Computer with Internet access

➡**Objectives**

- Witness the Civil War through the eyes of a child
- Share feelings about what Carrie Berry experienced during the war
- Gather facts about the lifestyle of children in this time period

6

Teaching the Civil War with the Internet

 # Procedure

1 Begin class by asking the students if they have ever kept a journal or diary. What do they write in their diary? Do they share it with anyone? If someone found their diary/journal 50 years from now, would the information help other people understand the history of that time? Today they are going to read a diary written by a ten-year-old girl from Atlanta, Georgia, who kept a diary during the Civil War.

2 Have students open the following Internet site.

Diary of Carrie Berry
URL: http://www.cee.indiana.edu/gopher/
         Turner_Adventure_Learning/Gettysburg_Archive/
         Primary_Resources/Berry_diary.txt

Teacher Note: You may want to print out this page before the class starts.

Read the diary entries with the students, stopping from time to time for classroom discussions. The following are some questions you may want to ask your students as you are reading:
- What frightened Carrie Berry?
- What was life like for her?
- Was she able to play and have much fun? Why or why not?
- What do you think it would be like to live under the conditions under which Carrie lived?
- How did she feel about school?
- What did she think about Yankees?
- Why were people driven from their homes?

3 Students will use Carrie's writing as a model to create their own Civil War diary. Every day after their Civil War lesson tell students to pretend they were actually living through the events they just studied. Students should attempt to incorporate things discussed in class that day into their diary. Students can share their diary entries with the rest of the class at the end of your Civil War unit.

Extensions

1 Have students write letters to Carrie Berry as if she were still alive. Ask them what they might say, and what they would want to ask her.

2 Open the following Internet site:

Civil War Diary and Letters of David Humphrey Blair
URL: http://netnow.micron.net/~rbparker/diary/index.html

This site contains the diary and letters of David Humphrey Blair. Students will be able to get another perspective of the war through this diary. The site includes voice clips in addition to written excerpts. Because of this, the teacher should visit this site ahead of time to download any necessary plug-ins. (This site is easy to use and includes clear instructions for the downloading process.) Have students react to his diary by writing a letter to David Humphrey Blair.

My Civil War Diary

Student name: _____

Class: _____ **Date:** _____

Date: _____

What's for Dinner?

Overview

Students will learn what life as a soldier was like during the Civil War. They will try foods of the time which could have been eaten by the soldiers and create their own meal.

Materials

- A computer with Internet access
- Supplies to create the recipes listed
- Index cards for receipe

Objectives

- Identify aspects of a soldier's life
- Taste foods from that period in time
- Create their own meal
- Follow directions for preparing food

Procedure

1 Students will learn about life as a soldier in this lesson, but will first need some background information about both Confederate and Union soldiers. This may include:

- Age range of the soldiers
- Training
- Weapons
- Food
- Living conditions while in the army

2 Tell students that they are going to make and taste some of the food that was typical of what the soldiers ate during the Civil War. You may want to contact parents to help volunteer to make some of the dishes. Depending on the age of the students, they may be able to prepare the different dishes themselves. Use the recipes that are included in this lesson at Brian Boyle's Bronx Bulletin Board to create the meal your students will sample.

Recipes and Food Information
URL: http://www.access.digex.net/~bdboyle/reenact/
        recipe.html

Have students think about dinner time for Civil War soldiers, considering such things as the conditions under which the men ate and what they think the food was really like then.

3 Once you have prepared the recipes, students can try the different foods. Have them discuss what they liked or disliked about them. Ask some of the following questions:
- Could you live on this for an extended period of time?
- Why do you think this food was served to the soldiers?
- How do you think you could have improved the meals?
- Do you think that the soldiers complained about the meals? Why or why not?

4 Have the students create a cookbook of their own of Civil War recipes. Tell them they are to pretend that they are camped out in the woods and only have certain food supplies. Generate a list of food they may have carried in their backpacks. Discuss whether it is possible to keep food cold and fresh.

 # Extensions

1 Open the following Web site:

Letters from an Iowa Soldier in the Civil War
URL: http://bob.usc.edu/civil-war-letters/home.html

This site contains letters written between Newton Robert Scott and Hannah Cone. Students can read the letters to interpret each person's view of the war. Have students write a letter to either person with questions they wish they could have answered, or comments they would like to make to these people.

2 Send home a copy of the corn muffin receipes for parents to try at home. This is a great way to get parents involved in the lesson.

Civil War Recipes

Student name: _____

Class: _____ **Date:** _____

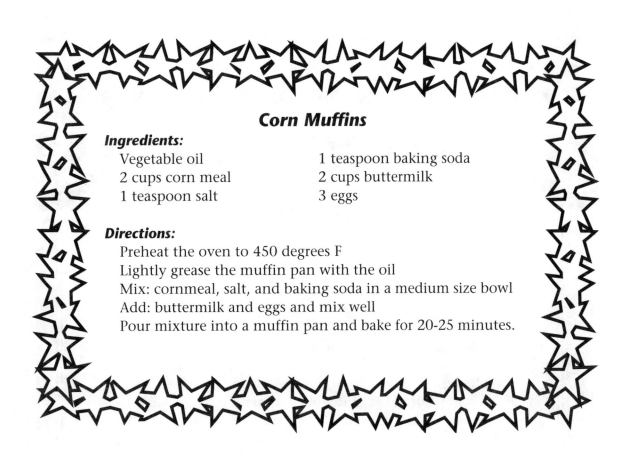

Corn Muffins

Ingredients:

Vegetable oil
2 cups corn meal
1 teaspoon salt

1 teaspoon baking soda
2 cups buttermilk
3 eggs

Directions:

Preheat the oven to 450 degrees F
Lightly grease the muffin pan with the oil
Mix: cornmeal, salt, and baking soda in a medium size bowl
Add: buttermilk and eggs and mix well
Pour mixture into a muffin pan and bake for 20-25 minutes.

Johnny Cakes

Ingredients:

1 cup yellow cornmeal   1 cup boiling water
1/2 teaspoon salt   1/2 cup milk

Directions:

Mix the cornmeal and salt. Add the boiling water, stirring until smooth. Add the milk and stir well in a medium bowl.

Grease a frying pan over medium heat. Drop batter onto frying pan and cook until golden brown (approx. 5 min.). Flip and cook other side in same manner.

Spoon Bread

Ingredients:

1 cup white cornmeal   4 eggs
1 teaspoon salt   1/3 cup butter
2 cups milk

Directions:

Preheat the oven to 350 degrees F. Mix the salt and cornmeal in a large bowl. Heat the milk in a sauce pan until little bubbles form at the edges and remove it from the heat (DO NOT BOIL). Stir in the butter until it melts. Add the milk to the cornmeal, and stir until smooth.

Beat the eggs with a fork and stir them into the cornmeal. Put the cornmeal mixture into a greased 8-inch square baking pan. Bake for 45 minutes.

Activity Sheet   What's for Dinner?

14

Soldier Recipe

Student name: _____

Class: _____ **Date:** _____

Ingredients:

_____

_____

_____

_____

_____

Directions:

_____

_____

_____

_____

_____

_____

_____

Civil War Medicine

Overview

This lesson will introduce students to medical care during the Civil War. Students will be responsible for collecting information and sharing it with their group members. In addition, students will role play and use props to create a "living wax museum" scene to demonstrate their understanding of the materials they have read.

Materials

- Computer with Internet access
- Classroom copies of activity sheet
- Bandages
- Various Civil War play props (if available)

Objectives

- Research information about medical care during the Civil War
- Share information with group members
- Create a living wax museum scene to show understanding of material

# Procedure

❶ Tell students that there must be a way of dealing with casualties and illness during war. Students will uncover information regarding the medical care given to the soldiers at the time. The class should be divided into teams of four people. Explain to your students that each member of the team will be responsible for one section of the entire team's research project.

❷ At this point, the teacher may want to pass out the "Summarization" activity sheets that accompany this lesson. Students should open the following Web site:

School of the Sick Soldier
URL: http://www.access.digex.net/~bdboyle/reenact/
sicksoldier.html

This site supplies information about the life of soldiers and the medical conditions at the time of the Civil War.

❸ Each person will be responsible for completing one of the activity sheets that accompany this lesson. Once the sheets are completed, students will be responsible for sharing their information to their classmates. In this way, they will get a more complete picture of the information presented at this site.

❹ Students will also be responsible for creating a living "wax" museum scene based on the medical information they uncovered at this Web site. Students will act as the life size "dummies" for their display. They will need to be able to summarize the information they researched and explain on command what their "wax display" exhibits. They should brainstorm (see activity sheet) suggestions on what their scene will be about, what it should look like, who has which part, and the how the display props will be made. You may need to help the groups get started.

5 Students can share their scene with another class when they complete their Civil War wax museum display. (It may take more than a day to complete.) Each group should have a narrator to explain the scene. It is the narrator's job to write a short script that will underscore the scene.

 # Extensions

1 Students may want to see more information about medical procedures during the Civil War. Use the following site to see pictures and descriptions of reenactments of medical sites during Civil War battles:

The Society of Civil War Surgeons
URL: http://www.civilwarsurgeons.org/

Have students write their reactions to the pictures and why they would not like to have those types of medical conditions today.

2 Have students write captions about what they think is occurring in the Civil War medical pictures at the following site:

Medical
URL: http://www.treasurenet.com/images/civilwar/civil010.html

Civil War Medicine

Student name: _____

Class: _____   **Date:** _____

Summarize your information in the boxes provided.

The U.S. Medical Department in the Civil War

> What was the department like at the start of the war?

> Describe a typical nurse.

> What would the uniforms of medical personnel include?

> What medical personnel would accompany a regiment? For what reasons would it differ?

> What was the difference between a yellow and red flag?

Civil War Medicine

Student name: _____

Class: _____ **Date:** _____

Summarize your information in the boxes provided.

In what ways did the surgeon maintain camp cleanliness?

What happened at sick call?

Infantry Regiment/ Sick Call and The Shirker

What might happen to a sick soldier?

What is a shirker?

What might the surgeon do to a shirker?

Activity Sheet   Civil War Medicine

Civil War Medicine

Student name: _____

Class: _____ **Date:** _____

Summarize your information in the boxes provided.

<table>
<tr><td rowspan="5">Symptoms, Disease, and Treatment</td><td>Why does it say that Civil War soldiers were unsophisticated in practicing medicine?</td></tr>
<tr><td>What were some of the main symptoms reported?</td></tr>
<tr><td>Why was "simple mindedness" common in regiments?</td></tr>
<tr><td>What were some common diseases seen by doctors?</td></tr>
<tr><td>Name three common treatments for illnesses.</td></tr>
</table>

Activity Sheet   Civil War Medicine

21

Civil War Medicine

Student name: _____

Class: _____ **Date:** _____

Summarize your information in the boxes provided.

> What would happen to the soldier that was wounded and could not carry on?

> What was the difference between the actions of a shirker and a respectable soldier?

The Wounded Soldier

> What was "manly behavior"?

> What were many soldiers afraid they would lose?

> What provisions were made for the mortally wounded soldier?

Civil War
Medicine

Student name: _____

Class: _____ **Date:** _____

Brainstorm your Civil War was museum scene in the space provided. The scene should be about medical treatment during the Civil War. You need to brainstorm your ideas, design the scene, assign the parts, create a narration script, and create the props for your wax museum scene.

Battle of the Iron Clads

Overview

This lesson will teach students about the Monitor and the Merrimack (The Virginia). Students will read background information and view pictures of the naval boats.

Materials

- A computer with Internet access

Objectives

- Compare/contrast sites on two naval boats
- Write a news story about the battle between the two boats

📖 Procedure

❶ Students will examine the battle of the Iron Clads in this lesson, but first, they need some background information on the Monitor and the Merrimack. Explain to the students that the Confederates were up against an advanced Northern navy. The Union was using its navy to run a blockade on the South. The South did not have a navy, so it ordered ships from England to run the blockade. The South coated the hulls of some of these ships with iron to protect them against fire or cannon balls.

One of the ships in the Confederate army sank near Norfolk, Virginia. The Confederates brought it to the surface and cut off the burned top half of the ship. Then the ship was coated with slanting metal plates. Holes for five powerful guns were cut in the sides of the roof. The ship was slow and moved in a clumsy fashion, but it sank several Union vessels. Once news of this ship reached the North, Lincoln and his cabinet began to discuss ways to combat this new warship. It was revealed that the North had been working on its own Iron Clad as the result of spying on the South.

❷ At this point the teacher may want to open the following Web sites. Each one has information about the ships, but the details are different.

The Duel Between the Monitor and the Merrimack.
URL: http://tqd.advanced.org/2944/monitor.htm

The Battle of the Iron Clads
URL: http://tqd.advanced.org/3055/graphics/experience/
     battles/ironclads.html

Both sites contain information on the Monitor and the Merrimack. Have students read the information, and have them note the differences between the two. Have students make predictions about which ship would win a battle if they went up against each other. They can defend their position with reasons and descriptions of the two boats.

❸ Next, distribute the "Newspaper Article" activity sheet that accompanies this lesson. Have students pretend they work for a newspaper at the time of the Civil War, and are responsible for writing an article. They will need to report on the events that took place and what they saw happen between the two boats. Tell students that a news article typically includes information that answers the following questions: who, what, where, when, why, and how. Have students read their newspaper articles in class. Remind students that they can create some of the information to add to the facts they have read at the sites.

 # Extensions

1 Have students create a Hyperstudio stack (or another multimedia presentation) about the naval ships of the Civil War. They can gain additional information at the following Web site:

The Civil War Blockade Runner Page
URL: http://members.aol.com/MaxDemon8/runner.html

Students can examine photos and diagrams of the boats to learn about naval blockade runners used during the Civil War. They can then compare these boats with boats of the past or present to discover how the U. S. Navy has changed over the years.

2 Open the following Web site to read about a battle that changed Naval warfare:

Confederate States Ironclad Ships
URL: http://www.geocities.com/Heartland/Park/2207/css.htm

Have students study the battle, and then design their own boats. Tell them it must be fast, protected, able to carry supplies or soldiers, and inconspicuous.

Newspaper Article

Student name: _____

Class: _____ **Date:** _____

Write an article about the clash between the Monitor and the Merrimack. Make sure you include all important information.

Taking a Ride on the Underground Railroad

Overview

Students will be introduced to the issue of slavery, and will access information on life as a slave, slavery statistics, and the Underground Railroad in this lesson.

Materials

- Computer with Internet access

Objectives

- List the main issues regarding slavery.
- Explain what the Underground Railroad was and how it functioned.
- Complete an activity sheet designed to help students understand the Underground Railroad.
- Share information with classmates.
- Supply reasons people were divided on the issue of slavery.

*Note: This lesson works best when students are split into groups of 2 or 3

 # Procedure

1 Introduce students to the idea of slavery. Explain that slavery in other countries started long before the United States was formed, but by the time the Civil War began, slavery had become the backbone of the South's economy. Tell students that the United States Constitution does not mention the words "slave" or "slavery." Ask the class how this affected a slave's rights. Go on to explain some of the following concepts:
- Slaves were seen as property without human rights.
- Slave laws were being enacted for runaway slaves.
- Quakers and abolitionists in the North were against slavery.

2 The following Web sites which will help them understand the hardships of the voyage from Africa to America, the magnitude of the slavery issue, life on a plantation, and the number of slaves at the time of the Civil War. The first will give an overview on the voyage from Africa to America, life on a plantation, and slave revolts.

Netscape: Afro-America@ Black Resistance . . .
Slavery in the U.S.
URL: http://www.afroam.org/history/slavery/main.html

3 Next, have students access this statistical site dealing with the following: the number of slaves in the South, families who owned slaves, the number of slaves on plantations, and investment information.

Selected Statistics on Slavery in the United States
URL: http://members.aol.com/jfepperson/stat.html

4 Explain that many Northern abolitionists strongly opposed slavery and formed the Underground Railroad to help free slaves in the South. Next, tell students that they will be exploring information about the Underground Railroad. Have students open the following site:

The Britannica Guide to Black History
URL: http://blackhistory.eb.com/

To access this site, you will need to sign up for a free seven-day subscription to Encyclopedia Britannica online. Click anywhere on the title Black History, on the next page click on 1619-1863, find the words Underground Railroad and click on them.

This site contains a brief history of slavery and the Underground Railroad. Have students use what they have read from each site to complete the "Underground Railroad" activity sheet that accompanies this lesson. Students should share the information on their activity sheet in a classroom discussion.

Extensions

1 Divide the class in half and hold a debate dealing with the topic of slavery. Appoint one side to debate slavery as necessary due to its economic importance. The other side can be abolitionist supporting the end of slavery. Students will need to research their topics to help support their issue.

2 Expose students to Negro spirituals. If you wish to modernize this activity, use the spiritual, "Swing Low, Sweet Chariot" by Eric Clapton. Tell students that the spirituals were sometimes used to pass messages to one another about escape plans and other things without the overseer's knowledge.

3 If you live near any "stations" on the Underground Railroad, take your students to visit. Some of these historic houses are now open to the public.

The Underground Railroad

Student name: _____

Class: _____ **Date:** _____

1. What was slavery?

_____

_____

_____

_____

2. How did the Fugitive Slave Act help to establish the Underground Railroad? To find this information click on the words "Fugitive Slave Act."

_____

_____

_____

_____

3. What was the function of the Underground Railroad?

_____

_____

_____

_____

4. How did slaves move through the Underground Railroad?

_____

_____

_____

_____

5. How many people were helped by the Underground Railroad?

_____

_____

_____

_____

6. Who was Harriet Tubman? To find this information click on the name "Harriet Tubman."

_____

_____

_____

_____

7. Click on the word abolitionist. Explain what an abolitionist was and name three. Do you think it was a great risk to be an abolitionist? Why or why not?

_____

_____

_____

_____

LESSON PLAN
Number 7

The Assassination of Lincoln

Overview

In this lesson students will learn about the assassination of President Lincoln and about his assassin, John Wilkes Booth.

Materials

- Computer with Internet access

Objectives

- Describe the events of the night of Lincoln's assassination
- Find facts about John Wilkes Booth
- Summarize what happened to John Wilkes Booth
- Design a reward poster for John Wilkes Booth

Procedure

1 You may want to begin this lesson by telling students that Lincoln had a premonition the night before he was shot. He told cabinet members that in his dream he was on a boat headed for a distant, misty shore. This was not the first time the President had had this dream.

The cabinet and the President disregarded the dream, and continued working on Reconstruction. They were deciding how the South would be brought back into the Union. Lincoln and his cabinet were discussing how to deal with the newly freed slaves now that the South had lost the war. They needed jobs, schools, and land, and Lincoln wanted to make sure that African Americans were treated fairly.

Early on the day Lincoln was shot, it had been decided that he and his wife would attend a show at Ford's Theater along with General Grant and his wife. Later that day, Grant decided not to go, and the president canceled his plans, too. However, he reconsidered knowing that his wife would be disappointed.

Lincoln was shot that evening during the play. The audience heard the gun fire and saw a man leap from the balcony onto the stage. They soon realized that the president was wounded. Lincoln died the next day in a small house across from the theater where he had been taken the previous night.

2 Have students open the following Internet site to gain additional information about John Wilkes Booth:

A History of John Wilkes Booth
URL: http://www.nps.gov/foth/booth.htm

Pass out the lesson plan worksheet that goes along with this site and have students complete the information. Once students have finished the work have them share their results with the rest of the class.

34

Lesson Plan   The Assassination of Lincoln
···
Teaching the Civil War with the Internet

3 At this point, you may distribute the worksheet entitled "Reward." Students will design a poster rewarding the capture of John Wilkes Booth. Have students share their ideas with the class and post the signs in the room.

 # Extensions

1 Have students explore Ford's Theater at:

Ford's Theater National Historic Site
URL: http://www.nps.gov/foth/index2.htm

Students will be able to click on links for photos of the theater, the derringer that Booth used, and maps of Booth's escape route. Have students create a crossword puzzle or word find of terms used to describe this event. For example:
- Derringer
- Booth
- Conspiracy
- Assassination

2 Tell your students that a controversy arose regarding John Wilkes Booth's death. Some people believed he may not have died at the barn that day, and the body discovered there was someone else's.

Open the following Web site:

The Positive Identification of the Body of John Wilkes Booth
URL: http://www.access.digex.net/~bdboyle/booth.txt

This site includes information about the autopsy performed on John Wilkes Booth. The information is not gory, and is fairly straight forward. It explains that the body's leg was fractured and it sustained other injuries that Booth would have received during his flight from Ford's Theater—including the bullet wound that killed him. This official autopsy positively identifies the body as that of John Wilkes Booth.

The History of John Wilkes Booth

Student name: _____

Class: _____ **Date:** _____

1. Where did Booth study acting in the mid 1800's?

_____

_____

_____

_____

2. How do you think Booth's move to Virginia influenced him?

_____

_____

_____

_____

3. Why did Booth enlist in the military in 1859?

_____

_____

_____

_____

4. How did Booth help the Confederate cause during the Civil War?

_____

_____

_____

_____

5. Describe the plot to capture Lincoln.

_____

_____

_____

_____

6. When the plot to kidnap Lincoln failed to work, what did Booth do?

_____

_____

_____

_____

The History of
John Wilkes Booth

Student name: _____

Class: _____ **Date:** _____

REWARD

Activity Sheet   The History of John Wilkes Booth

Take a Museum Tour on Life as a Soldier

Overview

Students will read information about the soldier lifestyle, create a diorama on a day in the life of a soldier, and complete a written activity to include with it.

Materials

- Construction paper
- Crayons
- Shoe box
- Scissors
- Glue
- Computer with Internet access

Objectives

- Describe items carried by a Civil War soldier
- Make a diorama that shows a scene from a soldier's life
- Write an explanation of the diorama from a tour guide's point of view

 **Procedure**

1 Explain to the class they will be going on a trip to a museum, but they will not be leaving the building. This will be a virtual trip through the computer. They will be viewing items that belonged to Civil War soldiers and reading information about them.

Have students open the site,

Atlanta History Museum
URL: http://www.atlhist.org/exhibit.htm

2 Click on Take a Virtual Tour of Gone for a Soldier, the Atlanta History Museum's original Civil War exhibit. Have the students read the information about each photograph and discuss:

- The quotes at the end of each exhibit
- How the quotes relay the emotion of the soldier
- How are the uniforms are different from today's
- Whether the soldiers are dressed appropriately for the seasons

3 Once your students have an idea of what life was like for a soldier, explain that they will be making a diorama that will show others what life was like as a Civil War soldier. They will be displaying their dioramas like museum exhibits so they will also need to accompany their work with a description. This may require some research.

The following sites can be used in addition for students to add information to their project.

The American Civil War
URL: http://homepages.dsu.edu/jankej/civilwar/civilwar.htm

Click on army life, click on Civil War slang, and view some of the slang words soldiers used. Have the students check to see if any are familiar and still in use.

Latest Additions to the Battle of Olustee WWW site
URL: http://extlab1.entnem.ufl.edu/olustee/new.html

Click on Authentic Uniforms and Accouterments and view the uniforms and items used by soldiers during the Civil War.

 # Extensions

1 Have students trace each other on bulletin board paper, draw Civil War uniforms on picture, and write a story about themselves as a soldier incorporating some of the soldier slang from the site. Hang the pictures in your diorama museum.

2 Have a soldier come in and talk to the class about what it's like to be in the military. Check to see if a student has a parent or grandparent who is a war veteran and would like to share some pictures and experiences.

Civil War

Grades 7-9

Abraham Lincoln

Overview

Using the Internet, students will find facts about Abraham Lincoln. This lesson will introduce students to Lincoln and his presidency during the Civil War.

Materials

- Computer with Internet access

Objectives

- Research biographical information on President Lincoln
- Work cooperatively to find information
- Give a brief overview of Lincoln's life and career

Procedure

Your students will go on a scavenger hunt to learn about Lincoln in this lesson. They will use the following Web site to find information about President Lincoln.

Supercomputing '94 - Abraham Lincoln
URL: http://sc94.ameslab.gov/TOUR/alincoln.html

Divide the class into six different groups. Each group is responsible for locating the information on its "Scavenger Hunt" activity sheet. Group members must then be prepared to share their findings with the rest of the class. After sharing the result with the class have each group assist in preparing a bulletin board that represents a time line in Lincoln's life according to what part of the "Scavenger Hunt" they were responsible for completing.

 # Extensions

1 Hold a mock election between Lincoln and Douglas. Have students find information about Lincoln's election opponent at the following site:

Illinois in the Civil War
URL: http://www.outfitters.com/illinois/history/civil/douglas-sa.html

2 Students can gain additional biographical information on President Lincoln by opening the following Internet site:

Encyclopedia Americana: Abraham Lincoln
URL: http://205.185.3.2/presidents/ea/bios/16plinc.html

3 Have students compare Lincoln to a more recent president. Address such issues as popularity, governing style, belief systems, and educational philosophy

Lincoln Scavenger Hunt

Student name: _____

Class: _____ **Date:** _____

Group #1

1. Where and when was Lincoln born?

2. Why did Lincoln's family move to Indiana?

3. What was Lincoln's opinion on education?

4. What did Lincoln's family do for a living?

Group #2

1. Why did Lincoln belong to the Whig party?

2. How did Lincoln feel about slavery at this point in his career?

3. What was Lincoln trying to accomplish as a politician?

Group #3

1. Why did Lincoln become a lawyer? What was his practice like?

2. List the members of Lincoln's immediate family.

3. Why did Lincoln oppose the Mexican War?

Group #4

1. What spurred Lincoln to run for office again?

2. What did Lincoln mean when he said, "A house divided against itself cannot stand"?

3. Even though Lincoln won the Lincoln/Douglass debates, why did he lose the seat in the Senate?

Activity Sheet Lincoln Scavenger Hunt

Group #5

1. Why was Lincoln nominated for President even though he was the party's second choice?

2. Who did Lincoln defeat to become President?

3. What happened by the time of Lincoln's inaugural address?

4. What happened on April 12, 1861?

Group #6

1. Who did Lincoln finally choose to take command of the efforts in the Civil War?

2. Why was Lincoln's popularity strained in his first term?

3. Why did Lincoln write the Emancipation Proclamation?

4. Who was John Wilkes Booth, and what role did he play in the Civil War?

Jefferson Davis

Overview

This lesson will introduce students to Jefferson Davis, the President of the Confederacy. Students will read information about the trial of Jefferson Davis that took place after the Civil War.

Materials

- Computer with Internet access

Objectives

- Explain Jefferson Davis's part in the Civil War
- Research information about the legal case against Davis after the war
- Identify some biographical information about Davis

Procedure

1 Give students some beginning background information on Davis such as the following:
- A brief biography
- Davis did not want the presidency
- He would have preferred to be a military general
- Davis was better educated than Lincoln
- Davis's career was more impressive than Lincoln's

2 Tell students that Jefferson Davis was arrested for treason and linked to President Lincoln's assassination at the end of the war. With the North and South torn apart, thousands of lives lost, and political upheaval in the country, this question remained: Why wasn't Davis convicted?

3 At this point, tell students that they will use the Internet to look for additional background information on the topic.

Students can open the following Internet site:

The Case Against Jefferson Davis
URL: http://www.ruf.rice.edu/~pjdavis/faq.htm#case

This site is a FAQ (frequently asked questions) about Jefferson Davis, and contains some biographical information about him. Have students scroll down to where it reads: "The Case Against Jefferson Davis." They can use this section of the Web site to look for more information about the case against Davis that will help them complete the Davis activity sheet.

4 Using the information gained in this lesson, have students hold a debate on the Davis case. Assign half the class to defend Davis, and the other half to prosecute him. Have your class decide whether justice was served in the Davis case, and if it was not served, what should have happened to him.

 # Extensions

1 Have students compare Jefferson Davis to President Lincoln. They can determine for whom they would vote and why, and then hold a mock election or campaign debate with candidates and speeches.

2 Have students create a mural of the home of Jefferson Davis using the following Internet site:

Beauvior
URL: http://www.beauvoir.org/

Students can click on links to find out about the history of the home and to view different photos.

The Case Against Jefferson Davis

Student name: _____

Class: _____ **Date:** _____

1. Describe why the case linking Davis to the Lincoln assassination fell apart.

_____

_____

_____

_____

2. Why were Northerners beginning to get anxious for the case to be settled?

_____

_____

_____

_____

3. Why did Jefferson Davis want to go to trial?

_____

_____

_____

_____

Activity Sheet   The Case Against Jefferson Davis

4. Why was the case against Davis dropped?

_____

_____

_____

_____

5. How do you think the public may have responded to the dropping of the case against Davis?

_____

_____

_____

_____

6. Do you think what happened to Davis was fair or unfair? Explain your answer.

_____

_____

_____

_____

7. If Davis had been found guilty, what do you think would have been a fair punishment? Explain your answer.

_____

_____

_____

_____

The Organization of the Armies

Overview

This lesson deals with the organization of the armies on both sides of the war. Students will learn why the numbers of an ideal troop varied from those of an actual troop. The life of an African-American soldier will also be explored.

Materials

- Computer with Internet access

Objectives

- Identify the basic structure of the armies of the North and South
- Hypothesize why many army units did not contain the ideal number of soldiers
- Explain the difference between the Infantry, Cavalry, and Artillery
- Summarize information based on the history of the African-American soldier in the Civil War

Procedure

1 Tell students that a call for soldiers followed the secession of the Southern states. As the number of volunteers increased, the North and South needed to organize and train the men for their armies. Most of the country's military leaders were educated at the same schools, so the North and South organized their armies in basically the same way.

The smallest unit was called a company. Companies were combined to form regiments. An infantry regiment consisted of 10 companies, while a cavalry regiment contained 12 companies. Regiments were numbered based upon the order in which they were formed and the state from which they came. For example, 28th Virginia.

2 At this point have students open the following Internet site:

Structure of the Confederate Army
URL: http://thinkshop.edu/adventure/Struct._Conf._Army.txt

This site features information about the organization of the Confederate armies. Distribute copies of the "Structure of the Armies" activity sheet, and have students use this site to complete the work.

3 This next site students will focus on the black Civil War regiments. This site will give a brief history of what is was like to be black and a part of the U.S. military during the Civil War. Students will also be able to view African-American Medal of Honor recipients.

History of African Americans in the Civil War
URL: http://www.itd.nps.gov/cwss/africanh.html#top

When students complete reading the site have them summarize the information they have read and make a mural to salute the people that received Medals of Honor.

Extensions

1 Have students read the following book: Charlie Skedaddle by Patricia Beaty. Have students view the history and photos of the Second Ohio Voluntary Infantry Regiment at the following site:

Second Ohio Volunteer Infantry Page
URL: http://members.aol.com/afs2ovi/2nd/history.htm

Then have students write their own story about a soldier, or design a monument in tribute to the Second Ohio Volunteer Infantry.

Structure
of the Armies

Student name: _____

Class: _____ **Date:** _____

1. An ideal brigade consisted of how many men? _____. This means the five
   regiments had about how many soliders each? _____. How does this total
   differ from the actual total of the brigades in Gettysburg? _____

   _____

   _____

   _____

   _____

2. Approximately how many men would be in the ideal corps? _____. Each
   Divison that made up the corps had about how many men? _____. How does
   this total differ from the actual total of the corps in Gettysburg? _____

   _____

   _____

   _____

   _____

3. How did this discrepancy between the ideal figures and the actual figures of Lee's army affect the battle of Gettysburg?

_____

_____

_____

_____

4. What is the difference between Infantrymen, Cavalrymen, and Artillerymen?

_____

_____

_____

_____

5. How would you feel if you were in charge of a company of men that sustained heavy losses and had to return to your hometown to tell the families?

_____

_____

_____

_____

6. If elected to lead your men into a battle would you be able to do it? Why or why not? How would it make you feel?

_____

_____

_____

_____

Activity Sheet   Structure of the Armies

**Activity
Sheet
11**

History of
African Americans
in the Civil War

Student name: _____

Class: _____ **Date:** _____

Use this information to help develop your monument of African-American Civil War
Medal of Honor recipients.

1. Define Emancipation Proclamation.

   _____

   _____

   _____

   _____

   _____

2. How many African-American soldiers made up the Union Army during the Civil War?
   Why was being part of the military important enough for runaway slaves to want to
   be a part of the military?

   _____

   _____

   _____

   _____

   _____

3. July 17, 1862 Congress passed two acts allowing the enlistment of African Americans with some resistance. Ironically a year later what event occurred that was a mile stone and validated the decision to allow African Amercians in the military?

_____

_____

_____

_____

4. Explain the phrase "Remember Fort Pillow."

_____

_____

_____

_____

5. What battle led to 14 out of 16 African-American soldiers receiving medals of honor? What change did this lead to in the Confederate army?

_____

_____

_____

_____

<table>
<tr><td>

LESSON PLAN

Number 12

</td><td>

Uniforms of the Civil War

</td></tr>
</table>

Overview

Students will learn about the uniforms and accouterments used by soldiers during the Civil War. The Web sites will provide background information and pictures of the uniforms and materials used by the soldiers.

Materials

- Computer with Internet access

Objectives

- Identify facts about soldier uniforms and materials
- Design their own uniform

📖 Procedure

1 You will need to supply some background information about the uniforms worn during the Civil War. Students need to know that the uniforms of the Civil War were anything but "uniform." Many soldiers wore the official Southern gray or the official Northern blue. However, others wore the uniforms of their state militia or borrowed uniforms from the Revolutionary War.

Uniforms were typically made of a heavy wool that was customary at the time. The wool was hot for the soldiers, but it was durable. They were often thankful for the warmth in the winter, but felt just the opposite during the hot summer months.

Many soldiers did not have any uniform at all. It was very common for soldiers to wear their regular clothes. This lack of uniformity made it difficult to tell what side a soldier was on in the heat of a battle. Therefore, it was not uncommon for soldiers to be killed by shots from their own side.

2 Have students open the following Web site:

Civil War Period Uniforms and Accouterments
URL: http://extlab1.entnem.ufl.edu/olustee/uniforms/
        uniforms.html

This site features a menu of choices regarding uniforms and accouterments used by soldiers during the Civil War. Distribute the activity sheet, and have students navigate through the links to answer the questions.

3 Allow students to share their results with the rest of the class when they have completed the activity sheet. Then, pass out the "Design Your Own Uniform" activity sheet so students can put their creative skills to work. They may choose to represent either side of the war, but remind them that they want the uniform to be clearly identified by their fellow soldiers. Have students share their designs and defend their choice of attire to the rest of the class.

# Extensions

1 Have students view the uniforms of the Confederate soldiers of theOrphan Brigade by opening the following site:

Uniforms of the Orphan Brigade
URL: http://www.rootsweb.com/~orphanhm/uniforms.htm

Have students read the descriptions and find the differences in the uniforms.

2 Have students create their own mess kit or "housewife." Have students share their kits with the rest of the class.

Uniforms
of the
Civil War Soldier

Student name: _____

Class: _____ **Date:** _____

1. From what type of cloth are most shirts made?

   _____

   _____

2. What would suspenders and braces be used for?

   _____

   _____

3. Name one major difference between the trousers worn during the Civil War and the trousers of today.

   _____

   _____

4. Examine the hats and determine which hat is your favorite. Explain why.

   _____

   _____

5. What do you think the "I" stands for on some of the buttons?

   _____

   _____

6. Why do you think the belt buckles are fancier for officers than for regular soldiers?

   _____

   _____

7. For what do you think the pigskin gaiters (worn above the shoe) were used?

_____

_____

8. What was held in the cartridge box?

_____

_____

9. What material was used in the making of most knapsacks?

_____

_____

10. Name four things that could be found in a "mess kit."

_____

_____

11. What was another name for a "sewing kit?"

_____

_____

12. How many men would sleep in a "wedge tent?" Measure out a 7ft by 7ft space in your room. Could you sleep in such tight quarters? Why or why not?

_____

_____

13. Why do you think canteens were so important to a soldier?

_____

_____

Activity Sheet   Uniforms of the Civil War Soldier

Uniforms of the Civil War Soldier

Student name: _____

Class: _____ **Date:** _____

Design Your Own Uniform

Activity Sheet Uniforms of the Civil War Soldier

Weapons of War

Overview

Students will become familiar with the artillery weapons and ammunition of the Civil War in this lesson. In addition, they will learn about the effects of artillery fire.

Materials

- Computer with Internet capabilities

Objectives

- Identify the weapons and ammunition of the Civil War
- Invent and sketch a diagram of a Civil War weapon
- Problem solve the issue of redesigning the weapon due to problems

Procedure

❶ Tell students that they will study the weapons used during the Civil War. Explain that the weapons used had to be mobile so soldiers could take the equipment from one site to another with relative ease. This was important to the success of a battle. Also a variety of new military equipment was developed and tested during the Civil War.

Students can go to the Civil War Artillery Weapons and Ammunition Web site:

The Civil War Artillery page
URL: http://www.cwartillery.org/artillery.html

❷ Distribute the Weapons and Artillery of the Civil War activity sheet, and have students explore the weapons and ammunition of the period by answering the questions.

❸ Next, have students pretend that they are the inventors of the weapons they have just read about used during the Civil War. After designing the weapons they were told that certain problems arose. Have the students in groups of four redesign the weapons while addressing the problems. When they are done they can present their ideas to the class of criticize. Allow students to disagree with some of the redesigning, and encourage everyone to give positive feed-back.

Note: Remind students that certain types of technolgy were not present at this time so their weapons must be era appropriate.

 # Extensions

❶ Have students create their own companies and design a drilling routine to prepare their company for war. Students can read and view information about the organization and drilling of an artillery battery at the following site:

Civil War Artillery-Organization and Drill site:
URL: http://www.cwartillery.org/adrill.html

❷ Students may be interested to learn what happened to the soldiers of a specific artillery battery. They can discover such information about the First Ohio Light Artillery Battery L at this site:

First Ohio Light Artillery Battery L
URL: http://www.geocities.com/heartland/5060/1stohio.htm

Have students write a newspaper article summarizing what happened to some of the soldiers in this Battery.

66

Lesson Plan   Weapons of War
....
Teaching the Civil War with the Internet

Civil War Weapons
and Artillery

Student name: _____

Class: _____ **Date:** _____

1. Draw a copy of the cannon and label the following parts: vent, knob, neck, muzzle, trunnion, muzzle face, chamber, and bore.

2. What does the term "gun" mean?

_____

_____

_____

_____

3. How did a "muzzle" loading cannon differ from a "breechloader" cannon?

_____

_____

_____

_____

4. Why were the spiral grooves in the barrel of a gun important?

_____

_____

_____

5. Why was bronze a poor choice to use in making guns? What was the problem with using cast iron for guns and how was the problem solved?

_____

_____

_____

6. What was the arc that was discussed in the article and how does it relate to the range that a cannon could shoot?

_____

_____

_____

7. How were the large cannons transported? Do you think this was a problem?

_____

_____

_____

8. What do you think it would be like to fire a large cannon?

_____

_____

_____

_____

Civil War
Magazine Article

Student name: _____

Class: _____ **Date:** _____

_____

_____

_____

_____

_____

_____

_____

_____

_____

_____

_____

_____

_____

_____

_____

A Soldier's Letter

Overview

Students will be able to witness specific battles of the Civil War through the eyes of some soldiers. Information about many battles is gleaned from letters written by soldiers who fought in them.

Materials

- Computer with Internet access

Objectives

- Identify major aspects of specific battles of the Civil War
- Examine the battles from the letters written by soldiers in the battles
- Reply to the soldier by writing a letter of response
- Identify how major battles affected the outcome of the Civil War

Procedure

❶ Begin this lesson by presenting background information on specific battles of the Civil War. This lesson may be duplicated for a number of battles, such as those listed below. We will use the battle of Fredericksburg as an example.

The teacher should first relay a number of background facts about the battle. Before the battle of Fredericksburg, the North was losing and demanding action from Lincoln and General McClellan. Lincoln decided to replace McClellan with General Burnside when he failed to chase the Confederates after the battle of Antietam.

Burnside was planning to take Lee by surprise at Fredericksburg, Va. Burnside moved his troops into place near Fredericksburg and awaited the delivery of pontoon bridges from Washington that would allow his troops to cross the river and attack Fredericksburg. Burnside did not know that the delivery would be delayed.

While Burnside was waiting for the bridges, Lee spotted his troops and began to move his men into Fredericksburg to reinforce it and protect it from the Union. Burnside's plan to surprise Lee had failed.

When the bridges arrived, Burnside attacked Fredericksburg in the face of Lee's troops. Traps had been set for Burnside's men. The casualties began to mount. By the end of the battle, he had lost 12,700 men out of his 106,000 soldiers. Lee would comment: "It is well that war is so terrible—we should grow too fond of it."

❷ At this point students should open the following Web site:

Howard's Papers, #355
URL: http://ils.unc.edu/civilwar/howard.html

This site will introduce students to a Confederate soldier named Isaac Howard. Have students read the letter that he wrote home to his father.

❸ Once the students have finished reading the letter from Howard, pretend that they are Howard's father and write back to Howard. They should include personal feelings and reactions to the battle at Fredericksburg. Below is a list of battles (each described in soldiers' let-

ters). You can assign individual letters for which students
may respond.
- Fort Sumter
- Manassas
- Hilton Head
- Fredrick, Md.
- Fredericksburg
- Yazoo River
- Chancellorvile
- Vicksburg
- Dalton
- Spotsylvania
- Raleigh

Each of the above letters can be accessed through the
Images of Battle Web site:

Images of Battle
URL: http://ils.unc.edu/civilwar/civilwar.html

Teachers: Ask students to simply scroll down until they
find the list of battles and soldier letters.

 # Extensions

1 Have students research a major battle of the Civil War and
write letters to their parents as if they were soldiers partic-
ipating in it.

2 Students can create a map of the battle of
Chancellorsville. This battle was considered the South's
finest hour. Information about this battle can be found at
the following site:

The South's Finest Hour: The Battle of Chancellorsville
URL: http://home.earthlink.net/~wandbpartin/

3 Let students design their own battle flag after exploring
the battle flags of the Confederate army at the following
site:

Battle Flags of the Confederacy
URL: http://www.livingston.net/aks/

72

Lesson Plan   A Soldier's Letter
....
Teaching the Civil War with the Internet

Points to Consider

Student name: _____

Class: _____ **Date:** _____

1. Why do you think General Burnside attacked Fredricksburg even though he knew Lee had discovered his troops?

_____

_____

_____

_____

_____

2. What new information about the battle did you gain from reading Issac Howard's letter to his father?

_____

_____

_____

_____

_____

3. What do you think Lee meant when he said: "It is well that war is so terrible—we should grow too fond of it?"

_____

_____

_____

_____

4. Considering that Issac Howard's letter was written on Christmas morning, how do you think his father felt reading the letter? What do you think it was like in the camp for the troops on Christmas morning?

_____

_____

_____

_____

Letter to a Soldier

Student name: _____

Class: _____ **Date:** _____

LESSON PLAN

Number 15

Surrender at Appomattox

 Overview

In this lesson students will examine Lee's retreat and surrender at Appomattox Courthouse. Students will consider the events of the day before as well as those on the actual day of the surrender.

 Materials

• Computer with Internet access

Objectives

• Identify reasons for Lee's surrender at Appomattox
• Supply a chronology of the events of the day before and the day of the surrender
• Summarize the information read by the teacher and on the site and construct a play focusing on the retreat and surrender of the south
• Design their own terms of surrender to be included in the play
• Discuss the ramifications of the South's loss

Teaching the Civil War with the Internet

 # Procedure

1 You will need to establish the background for this lesson. Explain the following to students and encourage them to take notes, so the information can be used in the play.
- General Grant's army was gaining in strength.
- Union troops were well supplied as opposed to the Confederate troops that lacked food and money.
- Confederate troop morale was low.
- Lee began to retreat after he realized he could not hold Petersburg against Grant.

When Lee realized he would not be able to hold Petersburg he ordered his troops to retreat to Appomattox Station where food and supplies would be waiting. Grant knew this retreat was important and moved to cut off Lee from the supplies. Grant's troops took a faster route into Appomattox Courthouse and seized the supply trains ahead of Lee.

2 Have students open the following Internet site:

Appomatox Court House, Lee's Surrender to Grant
URL: http://americancivilwar.com/appo.html

This site contains information about the events of the day before the surrender. Students should use this site to help them answer some questions on the "Prelude to Surrender" activity sheet.

3 Next, have them open the following site so they can complete the activity sheet: Lee's Retreat:

Appomattox Court House, April 9, 1865
URL: http://americancivilwar.com/statepic/va/va097.html

Allow students to openly discuss their answers about the surrender. In addition, have students brainstorm about the ramifications the surrender of the South may have had (e.g., Reconstruction, freeing of all the slaves and what to do with them, the rise of the KKK, etc.)

You may want to explain the irony of the surrender to your students. The surrender at Appomattox Courthouse was conducted at the house of Wilmer McLean, and was signed in his front parlor. This event is interesting because the Confederates used McLean's first farm as a meeting place at the beginning of the war, during one of the war's first major battles at Manassas Junction. McLean's home was bombarded by Union artillery. Eventually McLean sold his home and moved further South to get away from the war. It has been said that the Civil War began and ended at the home of Wilmer McLean.

4 As a final activity, students should start to construct the play. This can be done with the whole class or broken down into groups. Base the play on the information learned at the sites, on class discussions, and on what was read by the teacher. Students should also include what they think should have been in the terms of surrender that Lee was required to sign at Appomattox. You may want to video tape the play and share it with another class.

 # Extensions

1 Have students write a report (with visuals) about General Grant. Information about General U. S. Grant can be located at the following site:

Ulysses S. Grant
URL: http://www.whitehouse.gov/WH/glimpse/presidents/
       html/ug18.html

78

Lesson Plan   Surrender at Appomattox
....
Teaching the Civil War with the Internet

Prelude to
Surrender

Student name: _____

Class: _____ **Date:** _____

1. Describe the movements of both troops on April 8, 1865.

   _____

   _____

   _____

   _____

2. What did the Union troops do once they reached Appomattox Station?

   _____

   _____

   _____

   _____

3. How did the residents of Appomattox know that the Confederate troops were
   approaching?

   _____

   _____

   _____

   _____

4. Lee's Surrender to Grant

_____

_____

_____

_____

_____

5. Describe what happened on April 9, 1865?

_____

_____

_____

_____

_____

6. How did Lee react to the surrender?

_____

_____

_____

_____

_____

Activity Sheet   Prelude to Surrender

Terms of Surrender

Student name: _____

Class: _____ **Date:** _____

_____
_____
_____
_____
_____
_____
_____
_____
_____
_____
_____
_____
_____
_____
_____

Civil War

Grades 9-12

State Secession

Overview

Students will examine secession documents created by Southern states, and learn why some Southern states wanted to secede from the Federal Union. Students will then write their own declaration of secession.

Materials

- Computer with Internet access

Objectives

- Describe circumstances that led to states meeting on the decision of secession
- Identify why states chose to secede from the Union
- List common points of interest among Southern states
- Create their own declaration of succession

 # Procedures

1 Begin this lesson by setting the scene for your class with the following background information which you will need to research:

- State rights
- U.S. Constitution
- Southern states wanted to preserve their way of life.
- Anti-slavery movements were gaining in popularity.
- Lincoln becomes president.
- Southern states were very dependent on slave labor.
- The North was establishing personal liberty laws to counter the fugitive slave laws.
- States began to meet to discuss seceding from the Union.
- It was questionable whether new states entering the Union could be slave states.

Explain that it was common for states leaving the Union to write a declaration stating their reasons. Tell students that they will examine a few states' Declaration of Causes.

2 Have students open the following site:

Declaration of Causes of Seceding States
URL: http://funnelweb.utcc.utk.edu/~hoemann/reasons.html

This site contains the Declarations of Causes of Secession for Georgia, Mississippi, South Carolina, and Texas.

3 Divide your class into separate groups to work on the "Declaration of Causes" activity sheet that can be completed with the help of the above Web site. Assign a state to each group and then have a person from each group focus on a question on the Declaration worksheet. Allow students to share their results with the rest of the class. You may also want to discuss the similarities and differences between each states declaration.

4 As a follow-up activity, tell your students that your class is going to secede from the rest of the school. They can use the "Declaration of Secession" activity sheet to write a declaration of causes for the class's succession. This may be done in small groups to elicit a variety of ideas and opinions. Have each group prepare a presentation in which they explain their secession to the rest of the class.

 # Extensions

1 Students can read and analyze the Crittenden Compromise that was an attempt to resolve the secession crisis. Have students evaluate the compromise for strengths and weaknesses and determine why the compromise did not work. A copy of the compromise can be found at the following site:

The Crittenden Compromise
URL: http://sunsite.utk.edu/civil-war/critten.html

Declaration of Causes of Seceding States

Student name: _____

Class: _____ **Date:** _____

1. Name the major points of contention for the states that are seceding.

_____

_____

_____

2. What appears to be the most important issue that runs through each declaration?

_____

_____

_____

3. Why do the states feel it is important to secede?

_____

_____

_____

4. What are the states positions on state vs. federal power?

_____

_____

_____

Declaration of Secession

Student name: _____

Class: _____ **Date:** _____

_____
_____
_____
_____
_____
_____
_____
_____
_____
_____
_____
_____
_____
_____
_____
_____
_____
_____

Activity Sheet   Declaration of Secession

<table>
<tr><td>

LESSON PLAN

Number 17

</td><td>

A Letter
from Thomas Langford

</td></tr>
</table>

Overview

Students will gain a perspective on the war through the eyes of a soldier, and analyze a letter for information about the Civil War.

Materials

- Computer with Internet access

Objectives

- Describe life as a soldier
- Analyze letter for facts about Civil War
- Discuss contents of letter
- Discuss personal reactions to the letter and its contents

 **Procedures**

1 Open the following Web site:

Diaries, Letters, and Memoirs
URL: http://homepages.dsu.edu/jankej/civilwar/diaries.htm

Have students read the letter of a Civil War soldier named Thomas Langford who wrote letters home to his wife about the war. This correspondence is unique because it offers a first-hand glimpse into the life this soldier led while fighting for his side. Thomas discovers some interesting things about his fellow soldiers, the life of a soldier, and battle.

Have students read the correspondence, view his picture, and complete "The Letters of Thomas Langford" activity sheet. The activity sheet will prompt students to think about the humanistic side of the Civil War. It is important for the students to understand that both sides of the war were affected in similar ways.

When the activity is completed, allow students to share their reactions to the letters. You may want to facilitate the conversation by asking the following questions:

- Did anything surprise you in the letters?
- What was the most memorable item for you in the letter?
- How do you think his wife reacted to the letter she received?
- What do you think was the most difficult thing that Thomas was dealing with at that time? Support your opinion.
- How would you deal with the same situations if you were in Thomas's place and in his wife's place?

# Extensions

1 Have students create a memory book about soldiers of the Civil War. Have students open the following site:

Camp Moore Confederate Cemetery and Museum Home Page
URL: http://ourworld.compuserve.com/homepages/forrest64/

Suggested links at this site include the cemetery, a soldier's letter to Sarah, and the history of Camp Moore. Students can either assemble this memory book electronically (using Hyperstudio or Digital Chisel), or they can print the photos and write the information up to be assembled in a book format.

2 Take your students to visit a war veteran and discuss life as a soldier. The veterans hospitals welcome visitors. Before the visit you might want to have your students prepare with questions and a nice gift.

The Letters of Thomas Langford

Student name: _____

Class: _____ **Date:** _____

Summarize the contents of the letter in the first half of this activity sheet. Then write your personal reaction to the letters. Respond to the information making specific reference to some of the following items: soldier's life, witnessing of battles, emotional state, etc.

Summary:

_____

_____

_____

_____

_____

_____

Reaction:

_____

_____

_____

_____

_____

_____

_____

The Raid at Harper's Ferry

 Overview

Students will compare two first-hand accounts of the raid at Harper's Ferry, and identify differences in the accounts. In addition, students will examine how the accounts differ from that of a newspaper article about the same incident.

 Materials

- Computer with Internet access

Objectives

- Compare separate accounts of the raid at Harper's Ferry
- Outline similarities and differences in the various accounts
- Identify why Harper's Ferry played a role in the Civil War Era
- Hypothesize why accounts of the same incident are reported differently

 # Procedures

The students will compare three articles about the same event. First, they will examine the raid at Harper's Ferry through the eyes of two witnesses and then compare those accounts to what was printed in the newspaper. Students will need to pay close attention to details and maps at the different sites.

1 Distribute the "Harper's Ferry #1" activity sheet and have students open the following Internet site:

Recollections of the John Brown Raid by a Virginian Who Witnessed the Fight
URL: http://jefferson.village.virginia.edu/jbrown/boteler.html

This site includes a first-hand account of the raid at Harper's Ferry by a Virginian who witnessed the fight. Students need to read the information, take notes of important parts, and then open the following site:

Charles White's Account of the Raid at Harpers Ferry
URL: http://jefferson.village.virginia.edu/jbrown/vmhb.html

This site will take students to another first-hand account of the raid at Harper's Ferry. Have students read the information and compare the two eye-witness accounts of the same event. They will use these sites to help them complete the activity sheet that describes how the accounts are similar and how they differ.

2 When students have completed this part of the lesson, have them examine a copy of an article in the Harrisburg Pennsylvania Telegraph that appeared in October 1859. Students can access it at:

Harper's Ferry Tragedy—Mad Brown's Insurrection
URL: http://jefferson.village.virginia.edu/vshadow2/articles/
     hburg.so59.html#10.26.59a

Students will need to scroll down to the article—"Harper's Ferry Tragedy—Mad Brown's Insurrection." Have students read the article to decide how it differs from the first hand accounts they read. At this point, they should complete the "Harper's Ferry #2" activity sheet.

3 You should now encourage students to discuss the following ideas. You may wan to do this while incorporating a VENN diagram:
- Identify the similarities
- Identify the differences
- Discuss which account they feel is most accurate and why
- Hypothesize why the accounts may differ
- Show how the news article applies to today's reporting of events

Extensions

1 Students can compare the newspaper article in this lesson to that of other newspaper articles from different papers at the time of the Civil War. Have students determine differences between the articles and possible reasons for the differences. Such articles can be found at:

Civil War Newspapers: Coverage of John Brown's Raid
URL: http://jefferson.village.virginia.edu/vshadow/
jbrownnews.html

Harper's Ferry
Activity Sheet #1

Student name: _____

Class: _____ **Date:** _____

1. Briefly describe the event that took place at Harper's Ferry.

_____

_____

_____

2. In what ways were the two articles similar?

_____

_____

_____

3. In what ways were the two first-hand accounts of the raid different?

_____

_____

_____

4. Why do you think that the accounts may have differed?

_____

_____

_____

Harper's Ferry
Activity Sheet #2

Student name: _____

Class: _____ **Date:** _____

1. How did the newspaper account of the raid at Harper's Ferry differ from the two first-hand accounts?

   _____

   _____

   _____

   _____

2. Do you think that there is anything lacking in the way the newspaper report was completed? If so what?

   _____

   _____

   _____

   _____

3. How do you think the Harper's Ferry incident affected the start of the Civil War?

   _____

   _____

   _____

   _____

African-American Contributions to the Civil War

Overview

This lesson deals with African-American troops in the Civil War. Students will learn that African Americans played a significant part on both sides of the war, and will examine information about African American troops in the Civil War.

Materials

- Computer with Internet access

Objectives

- Discover major contributions of African Americans in the war effort
- Identify who led most of the African-American troops
- Explore prejudices among both the North and South
- Examine the accomplishments of two Colored Infantry Troops

Procedures

1 You should begin by establishing a background for students. Explain that the majority of the African Americans in the war fought for the Union and for their freedom, but many voluntarily fought for the Confederates.

Students should know that Black soldiers in the South fought for the Confederates to gain favor in their eyes, which in turn they felt would result in better treatment. Other soldiers were taken to the battlefield by their masters to serve them in war as they would have at home. While many of these slaves were unwilling, others were eager to help because they considered it their Christian duty to serve their masters in the war.

Many African Americans however, saw the war as a chance to escape to freedom. This was most prevalent in the border states. While the war was seen by Northerners in the beginning as the preservation of the United States, the African Americans saw the war as a slavery issue. Eventually the main issue of the war would be centered around slavery. As a result, many African Americans wanted to become involved in the Civil War.

2 The North began to organize African Americans into regiments. African Americans were allowed to fight, but few ever became officers. Most regiments were led by white officers and the Bureau of Colored Troops.

Have students open the following Web site:

United States Color Troops
URL: http://www.coax.net/people/lwf/usct.htm

This site will begin the students' exploration of the United States Colored Troops. Distribute the "United States Colored Troops" activity sheet, and allow students to use this site to begin their work. To finish the activity sheet, students will need to visit the following two Web sites:

Battle of Olustee and the Olustee Battlefield Site and Reenactment
URL: http://extlab1.entnem.ufl.edu/olustee/54th_MS_inf.html

Site Contained at:
URL: http://extlab1.entnem.ufl.edu/olustee/35th_USCI.html

❸ Students should discuss their results with the class. In addition, students may want to view a photo of the 54th reenactment group at the following site:

Battle of Olustee and the Olustee Battlefield Site and Reenactment
URL: http://extlab1.entnem.ufl.edu/olustee/pics/new_54th.jpg.

 # Extensions

❶ Have students summarize the story of a slave from the old South at the following site:

Black Southerners in the Old South
URL: http://odyssey.lib.duke.edu/slavery/oldsouth.html

❷ Have students illustrate the stories about slaves and their impressions of capture, passage across the Atlantic, living conditions, and emancipation at the following Web site:

Excerpts from Slave Narratives
URL: http://vi.uh.edu/pages/mintz/primary.htm

United States Colored Troops

Student name: _____

Class: _____ **Date:** _____

1. From where did most of the African Americans come to make up the Northern Regiments?

_____

_____

_____

_____

2. How did the Colored Troops help in the battle at Appomattox?

_____

_____

_____

_____

3. Describe the make-up of the 54th and how the 54th Massachusetts gained fame.

_____

_____

_____

_____

4. Why wasn't the First North Carolina Colored Infantry as famous as its counterpart, the 54th?

_____

_____

_____

_____

5. Black soldiers often received less pay than white soldiers. Would this have affected your decision to join the army? Why or why not?

_____

_____

_____

_____

6. Black casualties were often high when their troops saw battle. Why do you think this was so?

_____

_____

_____

_____

7. Why do you think that after the focus of the war shifted to the issue of slavery there were still African Americans fighting for the Confederacy?

_____

_____

_____

_____

Activity Sheet   United States Colored Troops

The Constitution of the Confederacy

Overview

Students will examine the Confederate Constitution of the Southern states for elements specific to the these states. They will identify how the Confederate Constitution created problems for Jefferson Davis. In addition, students will compare the Confederate Constitution to the U. S. Constitution.

Materials

- Computer with Internet access

Objectives

- Outlline the basic elements of the Confederate Constitution
- Compare/contrast the Confederate Constitution with the U. S. Constitution
- Identify the breakdown of powers in the Confederate States
- Show how the Confederate Constitution created problems for President Davis

📖 Procedures

❶ Begin this lesson by explaining that President Jefferson Davis faced many problems during the war such as lack of money and supplies and poor transportation. Davis and the Confederate Congress were not worried in the beginning because they believed England would buy their cotton and help finance the war for the South.

However, England was well stocked in cotton, and prices fell. In addition, Harriet Beecher Stowe had published *Uncle Tom's Cabin,* which helped the English people understand that the slaves were real people. England abolished slavery in her own country and began to view it as evil.

This was only the beginning of Davis's problems. The Confederate Constitution was established to make sure that the individual states had power over the central government. As a result, Davis did not have the power to fight a war. For example, Davis could not force states to pay taxes because of the Confederate Constitution. This meant that the Confederate army would be undersupplied and underfed.

❷ Have students open the following Internet site:

Constitution for the Confederate States of America
URL: http://www.geocities.com/BourbonStreet/1812/

which contains a copy of the Confederate Constitution. Distribute a copy of the "Constitution of the Confederate States" activity sheet, and have students complete the worksheet. It is recommended that students work in small groups to discuss the different aspects of the Constitution. There are three articles of the constitution and each article is split into parts. For purposes of the exercise, it may be advantageous to review some basic elements of the U. S. Constitution. You may want to provide your students with a copy of it.

Teacher's Note: the site (http://www.access.digex.net/ ~bdboyle/csaconst.html) gives a more detailed version of the Constituition of the CSA.

❸ Allow your students to discuss the results of their activity sheet with the rest of the class.

Extensions

❶ Have students write a persuasive piece of writing defending or opposing the Crittenden Compromise. Open the following site:

The Crittendon Compromise
URL: http://sunsite.utk.edu/civil-war/critten.html

Students will discover that this was the last effort to reach a compromise and resolve the secession crisis. Divide students into two groups to take the sides of the North or South and debate the compromise.

❷ Have students make oral presentations summarizing the Civil War papers of Jefferson Davis. Students will be able to read the papers by opening the following site:

Jefferson Davis Documents
URL: http://www.ruf.rice.edu/~pjdavis/docs.htm

Constitution of the Confederate States

Student name: _____

Class: _____ **Date:** _____

1. How were slaves counted when looking at a state's population for representation? Why do you think this was so?

_____

_____

_____

_____

_____

2. What did the Constitution say about slavery and run-away slaves?

_____

_____

_____

_____

Activity Sheet Constitution of the Confederate States

3. Who had the right to collect taxes?

_____

_____

_____

_____

_____

4. Describe several powers of the Congress.

_____

_____

_____

_____

_____

5. Describe several powers of the President.

_____

_____

_____

_____

_____

6. What was the length of term for a Confederate President?

_____

_____

_____

_____

Activity Sheet   Constitution of the Confederate States

7. Article III describes the judicial powers. Do you think they are similar or different to the U.S. Constitution's version of the judicial powers? Support your answer.

_____

_____

_____

_____

_____

8. How can the Confederate Constitution be ratified?

_____

_____

_____

_____

9. How do you think the Confederate Constitution helped to create the fall of the Confederacy?

_____

_____

_____

_____

Activity Sheet   Constitution of the Confederate States

<table>
<tr><td>LESSON PLAN

Number 21</td><td># Music of the
Civil War</td></tr>
</table>

Overview

This lesson will introduce students to the music of the Civil War. Students will compare and contrast songs of the North with those of the South. In addition, they will interpret the meaning and messages in those songs.

Materials

- Computer with Internet access

Objectives

- Give reasons for the importance of music to the Civil War troops.
- Analyze two songs from the Civil War.
- Identify attributes that made a song a Union song or a Confederate song.

📖 Procedures

❶ Explain to students that music during the war was very important to the morale of the Union and Confederate troops. In fact, musicians were not engaged in battle. As a result, recruiters were not concerned about the age of enlistees. This meant that many of the musicians (drummers especially) were children. Although children and musicians were not to be engaged in battle, enemy bullets did not discriminate between men and children. The musicians were in charge of keeping the morale of the troops high, and would help soldiers find their regiment during a battle.

Open the following Web site to see a copy of the song "Music in Camp" by John Reuben Thomas:

Music in Camp
URL: http://home.erols.com/kfraser/campmusc.htm

Have students identify elements in the song that suggest the importance of music to the soldiers in the war.

❷ Next, open the following site for songs played by the Union bands:

Songs of the Union
URL: http://home.erols.com/kfraser/usongs.htm

Download or print a copy of the words for a Union song.

❸ Now open:

Songs of the Confederacy
URL: http://home.erols.com/kfraser/csongs.htm

for songs played by Confederate bands. Download or print a copy of a Confederate song like "Dixie's Land" by Daniel Decatur Emmett. Make copies of each song for your students. Have them analyze the songs to find out why they were played for the troops on each side. Have students use the attached "Song Attributes" worksheet to list their ideas to share with the class.

Extensions

1 Have students try their hand at writing the lyrics for a Union or Confederate Civil War song. Have students analyze other songs from the Civil War before they try writing their own lyrics. Opening the following Web site:

Corinth Information Database Version 1.3
URL: http://www2.tsixroads.com/Corinth_MLSANDY/
    songsciv.html

Students should know that the songs reflected the people's feelings of the war and war efforts. Students could take a controversial topic of today and express a specific view point in the lyrics.

2 Students can download sound clips of Civil War songs at the following Web site:

USS Monitor: Battle of the Ironclads Original Music
URL: http://www.evansville.net/~mmd/music.html

Have students use Digital Chisel to create an electronic song book of Civil War music. Have students compare the songs and determine the references to either the Union or Confederate sides and make note of the references in their song book.

Music of the Civil War

Student name: _____

Class: _____ **Date:** _____

Attributes of a Union Song	Attributes of a Confederate Song

Women in the Civil War

Overview

This lesson details some of the efforts of women, such as Rose O'Neal Greenhow who helped the Confederates in the Civil War. Students will need to make a decision about whether they believe she helped or hindered the women's rights movement that was emerging in the United States at this time.

Materials

- Computer with Internet access

Objectives

- List ways women participated in the Civil War
- Identify how Rose O'Neal Greenhow contributed to the Confederate effort
- Summarize two articles about Rose O'Neal Greenhow
- Decide whether Rose O'Neal Greenhow helped the women's movement or hindered it
- Report on another woman from the Civil War period

 # Procedures

1 Students need to understand that the Civil War was considered a white man's war. Women were not expected to do much more than make bandages or become nurses. However, many wanted to do more. A few women actually disguised themselves as men so they could fight in battles. Some women did this to be with their husbands; others felt strongly about the war.

This lesson will be about one particular woman and her efforts to help the Confederacy in the war. Before introducing Rose O'Neal Greenhow to your students, you should briefly talk about the battle of Bull Run. Describe the battle, its importance in the war, and the outcome. This is vital because Rose O'Neal Greenhow played an important role in the battle.

2 Have students use the following two Web sites to complete the "Rose O'Neal Greenhow" activity sheet:

Rose O'Neal Greenhow Papers
URL: http://scriptorium.lib.duke.edu/greenhow/

3 When the activity sheets are completed, have the students share their ideas with the class. Then have students discover and report on another woman from the Civil War. They should use the Internet to locate information to present to the class. Have them explain how the person they have chosen relates to the burgeoning women's rights movement that was beginning in the United States at the time.

Extensions

1 Have students try to create a personality profile of Rose O'Neal Greenhow. Students can view actual letters written by Rose O'Neal Greenhow and gain additional insight about her by opening the following site:

Rose O'Neal Greenhow Papers: An On-line Archival Collection
URL: http://scriptorium.lib.duke.edu/greenhow/roseindex.html

2 Have students create a fictional diary surrounding a particular battle or event of the Civil War. To get students started, have them read the diary of a woman who lived in Chambersburg, Pennsylvania, during the siege on Gettysburg. The information is located at the following site:

Diary of Rachel Cormany
URL: http://jefferson.village.virginia.edu/vshadow/rcormany.html

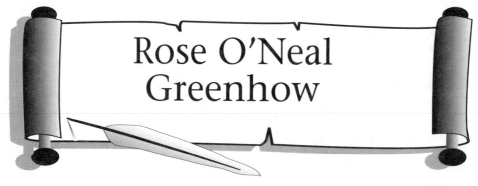

Rose O'Neal Greenhow

Student name: _____

Class: _____ **Date:** _____

1. Write a brief synopsis of the material you read.

_____

_____

_____

_____

_____

2. Why do you think her book was a best seller in the British Isles?

_____

_____

_____

_____

_____

_____

Activity Sheet   Rose O'Neal Greenhow
....

3. How do you think Rose O'Neal Greenhow was able to get the Union secrets?

_____

_____

_____

_____

_____

_____

4. Do you feel that she helped or hindered the women's movement in the United States and why?

_____

_____

_____

_____

_____

_____

Activity Sheet   Rose O'Neal Greenhow

117

Notes

Notes

Notes